TOCCATA
from Sonata No. 6 in A

P.D. Paradisi
(1707-1791)
y David Marlatt

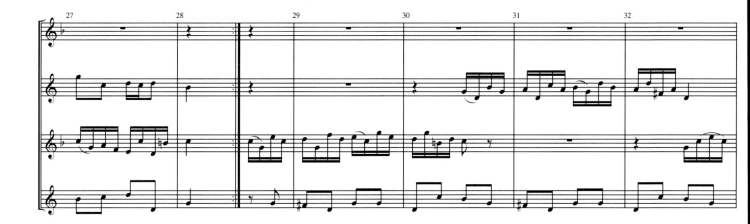

TOCCATA
from Sonata No. 6 in A

B♭ Soprano Saxophone

P.D. Paradisi
(1707-1791)
Arranged by David Marlatt

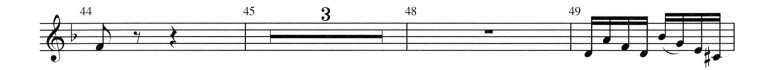

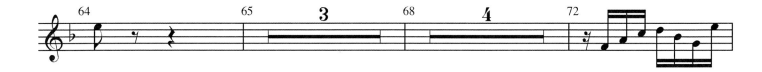

Eb Alto Saxophone

TOCCATA
from Sonata No. 6 in A

P.D. Paradisi
(1707-1791)
Arranged by David Marlatt

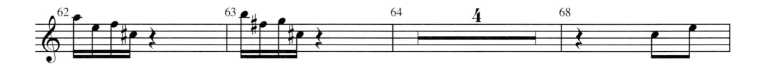

B♭ Tenor Saxophone

TOCCATA
from Sonata No. 6 in A

P.D. Paradisi
(1707-1791)
Arranged by David Marlatt

Allegro Moderato ♩= 84

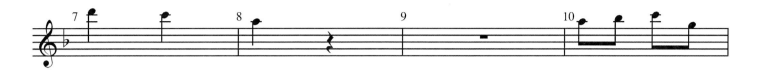

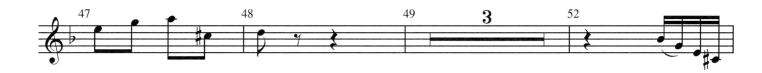

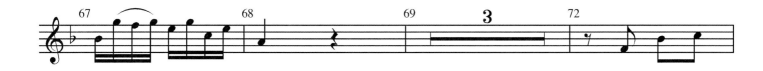

molto rit.

TOCCATA pg. 2

TOCCATA
from Sonata No. 6 in A

Eb Baritone Saxophone

P.D. Paradisi
(1707-1791)
Arranged by David Marlatt

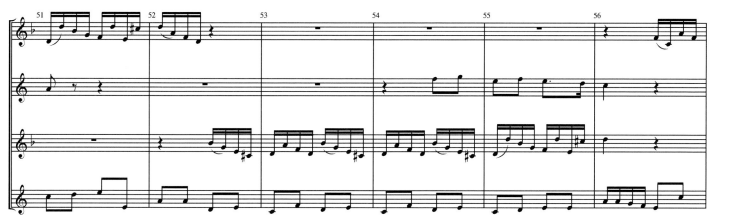

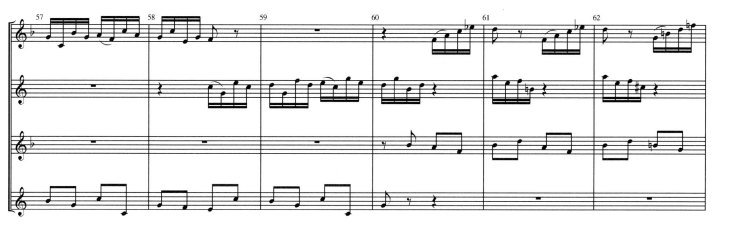

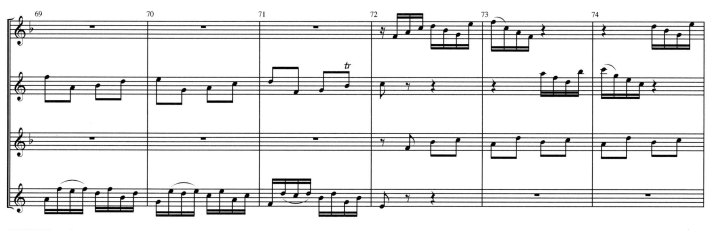

TOCCATA pg. 3